Wanderlust Emotions

SUKHMANI LUBANA

India | USA | UK

Presentation by *BookLeaf Publishing*

Web: www.bookleafpub.com

E-mail: info@bookleafpub.com

ISBN:9789360946890

First edition 2024

DEDICATION

This book is dedicated to .....YOU.

People who are reading this book, it is written for you and dedicated to you and your emotions.

ACKNOWLEDGEMENT

In the tapestry of life, where emotions intertwine and stories unfold, I am humbled to embark on this poetic journey. "Wanderlust Emotions" is not merely a collection of verses; it is a testament to the myriad experiences that shape our existence. As I reflect on the creation of this book, I am profoundly grateful to those who have accompanied me on this voyage.

To my family, whose unwavering love and support have been the bedrock of my endeavors, thank you for believing in me and inspiring me to chase my dreams.

To my friends, the kindred spirits who have shared in both laughter and tears, your presence has enriched my life in countless ways. Your encouragement have been a source of strength and joy.

To the muses who whispered in my ear and the emotions that stirred within my soul, thank you for lending your voices to these pages. Each poem is a tribute to the depth and complexity of human experience, a reflection of the moments that have left an indelible mark on my heart.

To the readers who embark on this journey with me, thank you for your curiosity, your empathy, and your willingness to embrace the beauty of language and emotion. May these verses resonate with you, offering solace, inspiration, and a glimpse into the vast landscape of the human spirit.

And finally, to the countless poets, writers, and artists who have paved the way with their creativity and passion, thank you for your inspiration and guidance. Your words have lit the path before me, illuminating the way forward with their brilliance.

With heartfelt gratitude,

Sukhmani Lubana

PREFACE

I welcome you to this beautiful journey of emotions. This collection of 18 poems marks the inception of my journey into the realm of poetry—a journey fueled by a passion for language, imagery, and finding solace in it

Within these pages, you will find echoes of joy and sorrow, love and longing, hope and despair. Each poem is a reflection of moments captured in time, woven together with threads of introspection and imagination. You will relate with each poem and some of them are told in a story format. Every poem has a deep connection with real life which will help you to connect to it.

As you delve into this anthology, I invite you to immerse into this beautiful journey together. May these verses resonate with you, inspire you, and awaken within you a newfound appreciation for the artistry of words.

With gratitude for your presence on this poetic voyage,

Sukhmani Lubana

SMILE

Smile is a communicable disease,
Which you catch like a cricket ball,
When somebody smiles at you,
You start smiling too.

I remember my last big smile with my friends,
We laughed at illogical content.
But you don't think that's what friends are for,
Making you smile even if you don't have a hard
reason.

Smile has many forms and names,
We smile when we achieve something,
We smile when we make fun of something,
We smile when we like somebody,
We smile when we tease someone,
And so on.
But most importantly the best smile is
when it comes from our hearts
 and we find peace in that.

People always carry big smiles even when they
don't want to,
And with no time, they feel happy again,
That is the power of a smile.

And you should smile too 😊
Because a smile makes us a beautiful person.

THE FIRST SIGHT

The first sight of you stopped my heartbeat,
I forgot the way I was going for a meet,
I Didn't blink for a second,
When I saw you in that moment.

Your laugh reminded me of my own time,
When I was happy with my mind,
Thought of the time made me smile,
Wondering what kind of is this sight.

That one moment hit me so high,
I felt joy, peace, and happiness all at one time,
In your eyes, I found my solace,
For me you became flawless.

In your eyes, I saw love and peace,
No wonder I can't get off at ease,
With hope to see you again sometime,
I made a move after looking at that beautiful
sight.

THAT FRIEND

It's been a long time,
I have seen you my friend,
Holding on to memories,
The time we have spent.

I remember us as soulmates,
People called us siblings,
I don't know why we did that fight,
Still searching you with my every sight.

Maybe I will never tell you this feeling,
I miss doing 3rd wheeling,
Our laughs, texts, fights, scooty-drive,
Everything I miss, can't deal with this deprive.

Wish I could do time travel,
To feel that one day again,
Where we didn't know the meaning of stress,
Where we can talk again.

Hoping to see you next time,
Where we can still be mad like last time,
The worst part that made my mind blew,
 A journey from friends to not knowing you.

THIS WORLD

The words that make us fly high,
They never let our thoughts dry,
Something that begins so harsh,
Help us learn the world better far.

People drive us crazy with comments,
But they make us ready for an event,
I wonder why we don't see that line,
That makes us better than the world that climbs.

How far we have gone from kid to adult,
That is leading us to a better world,
Overcoming fears, cliches, and dark light,
But still, we are making a place full of our vibe.

Stress, anxiety, and depression can't overtake
our minds,
This world has to offer a full worthy life,
I hope this helps you understand the fact,
Life is too short, so let us don't comment.

IT HURTS

When you say you don't feel for me,
It hurts.
When you say I can't help you heal,
It hurts.
When you say I am not real,
It hurts.

The thought of losing you makes my heart
wrench,
You feel nothing for me makes me low wench,
Talking to you to get closer or
 being jealous of another person in your life,
It makes me pathetic and drenched.

I hate me for loving you so hard,
Love that consumes I thought is the way to your
heart,
Waiting for your text feels me unwanted,
Maybe I am not the person you always wanted.

After all of that, I still feel a stretch,
Not wanting to lose you this quick,
Finally, when I saw someone taking my place,
I hate I wanted to burst,
cause it hurts.

UNSPOKEN

When the time is also testing,
Your choices of life,
You held yourself together,
For a single point of time.

Worthy of living a full life,
Once decided to demolish,
your broken parts of life,
collided to abolish.

Thought of giving up on life,
For things that happened through this time,
I promptly saw a child on the way,
Without legs working on a pave.

A light of ray suddenly appears,
In form of a chime way,
Your decisions should be given,
A chance of a second name.

All things fall into a point,
Where he was given a second life,
Chose to speak about this part ,
Which is in some hidden spot of life.

THAT WALK

We were walking in the mountains,
Holding each other hands,
 We trembled because of the wind,
In our beautiful dreamland.

We smiled at each other,
While holding our hands,
Sat on a desk near the castle,
And suddenly started the rain in marshland.

we were dancing in the rain,
while holding that moment,
we couldn't believe it was true,
met after so long of the war event.

We talked for hours and hours,
And laughed hard with tears in our eyes,
There was tranquility in that noise,
We found solace by spending together time.

Suddenly someone walked to my room,
I was shocked after hearing that news,
War is not yet over and is extreme,
Then I got to know that was a dream.

FRIENDS

I have found some weird friends in my life,
They all do some things that cause trouble to
invite.
They slay in doing stupid things,
And every day they have new ways of teasing.

Teasing, annoying, beating only friends have
that license,
But still, they say they don't like violence.
If any one of us gets into any problem,
Friends make sure to solve it with any realm.

Sitting at the last benches and laughing like a
fool,
Making faces, bunking, everything was cool.
Remembering those moments makes my heart
wrench,
Want to hug you guys and sit again on that
bench.

Some people got to fall in love,
But some of them got in trouble.
Friendship and love are 2 different words,
But the roots and relations of it are similar.

We don't know when will we meet again,
But we will remember those moments again and
again.
Our story was not only until this,
but new turns will come with new bliss.

FAMILY

When no one believes in us,
No one feels for us,
No one have faith in us,
Family supports us.

Family surrounds us with care,
They believe in our dreams,
Even if we don't take their advises seriously,
Family always stood for us as a beam.

Family is like a special curtain,
That saves us from UV rays,
But provides us sunlight in times of need
In different ways.

Family gives us a different form of love,
Without any return, they want us just to be
happy,
They want our success, happiness, joy,
And never mind when we are snappy.

At one point of time in life,
We feel the family is not understanding,
But always remember only family understands
us

More than ourselves.

I MET YOU

I used to hide my smile,
I used to not talk to people,
I used to not look at people,
Then I met you.

U changed me altogether,
U helped me to talk with people,
U made me smile every day,
I am glad I met you.

You cared for me,
You liked me the way I couldn't,
You knew me more than myself,
I wonder how I met you.

You did bring the best out of me,
You taught me to be confident around people,
you were the only one who never judged me,
I felt safe around you the time I met you.

I used to ask how I met a person like you,
Doing everything for me with no hope of any
return,
How can someone be so selfless,
But I understood and loved myself too,

After I met you.

NOTHING IS PERMANENT

In this world of ownership,
Where people fight for their rights,
Have to understand one simple thing,
Nothing is permanent.

Maybe it feels today, everything is mine,
Maybe it seems you are doing fine,
When you route to the next part,
Everything starts falling apart.

Where people seem yours,
You don't want to share your loved ones,
You want to feel important,
But nothing is permanent.

The love you are feeling,
The emotions that are drowning,
Everything is temporary,
You will feel it eventually.

You will only remember sometimes,
Where your soul was happy as flying,
Things you love will only matter,
Because nothing is permanent.

A CUP OF TEA

A sip of tea surrounded by heaven,
It makes me think it is Evan,
The smell of it soothes the mind,
And by drinking, I get blind.

When your world starts crumbling down,
And nothing is working out,
Leave everything aside,
Make a cup of tea and declutter your mind.

After sipping your tea,
You will feel free,
Flying in the clouds,
And wandering where you want to be.

Tea is like a worship to body and soul,
Helps to heal your mind for long,
You catch the energy instantly,
With a mind-boggling mode.

There is a comfort in it's fragrance,
There is a solace in it's taste,
Cherish the moment of being free,
By making a cup of tea.

UNEXPECTED

I was stuck in the crowd,
You made me different.
Dreams got diminished,
You made a path for me.
I forgot my own identity,
You made me realize it.

Colour and beauty is an illusion,
Life is a short story,
What kind of friendship do we have,
One is lock and the other one is key.
We fight like dog and cat,
But still together at the end

Everybody has a different soul,
But ours is one.
When we met for the first time,
Never thought we would be so important to each
other.
Starting from 2 cups of tea,
Spending life together.

Life's desire has been achieved,
got a sister like you with creepy weep.
We make nicknames for people,

And laugh together.
We have a long way to go honey,
To achieve everything.

THE MOON

The way the moon shines,
You shine like that spirit.
The way the moon smiles,
You sparkle like a skylight.

The way the moon carries its black spots,
In the same way, u carry your flaws.
The way the moon hides its water,
You hide your pain.

The way the moon has dark shades,
You had a dark past.
The way the moon is valued,
You also have worth.

The way people adore the moon,
I adore you.
The way people can't breathe on the moon,
I can't breathe without you.

MY HAPPY PLACE

When I am overwhelmed,
 I go to my happy place.
When I am cheered,
When I feel sad,
When I feel overjoyed,
When I cry,
When I can't breathe,
When u can't deal with events,
When I want to make some decisions in my life,
When I have to talk to myself,
When I have to understand something,
When I want to talk to somebody,
When I have to share something,
When I achieve something,
When I assume my victory on my own,
When I don't agree with things,
When I have to prepare myself before talking to
my parents,
When I have to do some self-care,
When I have to face the reality,
When I have to reflect on something,
Whenever I feel emotional,
There's just one place to go
My happy place.

WANDERING THOUGHTS

When we were all children,
Our goals were different.
We knew only some areas,
And thought that was the end.

We didn't know there was a whole world
waiting eagerly for us to explore,
to give it a new shape
and make love it more.

Any other day we thought of being artistic,
And someday we thought to be mystic,
Then we wanted to be doctors, lawyers, or
bookish,
When we became adults, we went realistic.

Everything is an illusion,
We have to keep it aside.
What we feel is the most important,
Where our heart lies.

Do what keeps you sane,
Which helps you to weight gain,
Which will keep your peace and reality in check,
That is going to be the best

RESILIENCE

When everything is under the night,
You seek out your moment to shine,
Maybe nobody will understand today,
But you will eventually reach your rise.

When you find nothing is better off,
Still, there's a chance for growth,
Maybe someday everything will be fine,
When you will reach your sublime.

When finishing off tasks will not be a daily
routine,
The world will crumble down to a sinking ship,
Doing your routine work is the least you have
got,
You are just a single step behind to start.

I know you will feel lazy and not doing anything
at the time,
But this is where you have to shine,
Focus on the work and person you want to be,
Because that's where your resilience lies.

HOPE

A word that sticks with us forever,
We hope from our birth to deathbed,
It not only helps us to think better,
But also to see the universe differently.

We hope for the best,
We hope for the best career,
We hope for the eternal love,
We hope for the forever friendship,
And we hope for what not.

It sounds as a word,
But it provides purpose to our lives,
We work hard daily because of hope,
We wake up daily because of hope.

Hope tells us how to live a life,
Why to live a life,
And for what and whom to live a life.
It is a universal emotion for everyone.

Hope brings us happiness,
Cheers us during our low times,
And remind us of our worth.

It is not just a word,
HOPE IS AN EMOTION.

www.ingramcontent.com/pod-product-compliance
Lightning Source LLC
LaVergne TN
LVHW021335200726
843509LV00014B/2544